# Here's One I Wrote Earlier
# Year 6

# Here's One I Wrote Earlier

# Instant resources for modelled and shared writing

# Year 6

## Gill Matthews and Gill Howell

First published in 2001 by Learning Matters Ltd.

© Gill Matthews and Gill Howell

*British Library Cataloguing in Publication Data*
A CIP record for this book is available from the British Library.

ISBN 1 903300 27 4

Cover and text design by Topics – The Creative Partnership
Project management by Deer Park Productions
Typeset by Anneset, Weston-super-Mare, Somerset
Printed and bound in Great Britain by Ashford Colour Press, Gosport, Hants.

Learning Matters Ltd
58 Wonford Road
Exeter EX2 4LQ
Tel: 01392 215560
Email: info@learningmatters.co.uk
*www.learningmatters.co.uk*

# Contents

# Introduction

*Here's One I Wrote Earlier,* as its name suggests, offers a substantial bank of examples of writing that you can use in modelled and shared writing sessions.

Demonstrating how to approach a particular piece of writing, or an aspect of the writing process, is an extremely effective teaching strategy. However, to think of ideas and to prepare resources for these sessions can be time consuming – and often challenging.

The examples provided here range from brief story extracts to blurbs, from biographies to historical reports. These examples are aimed at different stages of children's development – from a planning frame to an outline draft and then to a model text – so you can use them to take children through the whole writing process.

## What are modelled and shared writing?

Modelled and shared writing take place during the whole-class session of the literacy hour. They are used to demonstrate specific skills and strategies used by writers. Modelled writing involves the teacher in 'creating' the piece of writing in front of the class. Shared writing is collaborative – the children make suggestions for content, choice of vocabulary, sentence construction, etc.

Children often think that experienced writers write perfectly all the time. It is important therefore, that when using both teaching strategies, that you talk to the children about how you write e.g. rehearsing sentences out loud before writing them down, explaining choices of particular words and phrases, discussing possible spelling options. It is useful sometimes to make mistakes – and to demonstrate how to edit and improve a piece of writing as you write.

To keep the children interested during modelled and shared writing, you could involve them by using interactive techniques (e.g. asking questions, giving quick individual writing tasks on the whiteboard, taking time out for discussions, asking the children to come out to the front to write, etc.). Make sure that all the children can see – and reach – the writing surface. When appropriate, write on paper rather than a wipe-clean surface as this will mean the writing can be returned to for further work.

## How to use this book

There are two ways to find appropriate writing examples in this book:

- Page v lists the contents of the book by literacy focus. Use this page to find, for example, samples of story genres or instructions.

- The grid on page ix lists the teaching objectives covered and the relevant examples of writing.

The examples are organised by term and in groups that take you through the development of a piece of writing. **All the examples in the book may be photocopied**. Some examples have been annotated so you can use them to focus on specific teaching points (for example, pages 9 and 10, 16 and 17, 22 and 23, etc.).

Each page is organised in the same way to help you find your way around each example quickly and easily. Each example is prefaced by contextual information and is linked clearly to the National Literacy Strategy (NLS) teaching objectives.

You'll also find suggested writing activities after each example:

 This indicates suggestions for teacher-led activities when working with the whole class.

 This indicates suggestions for activities the children could complete independently, either on their own, in pairs or in groups.

You may wish to remove the activities section at the bottom of the page and then enlarge the page, or make copies for use on an OHP. In some instances, you could give copies to the children for them to work on independently. Equally, you could use them for ideas and present them as if you had written them earlier!

## Stimulus material

Wherever possible, the topics chosen for writing for each term have been linked to provide continuity. The examples are based on the identified range of texts for reading and writing in the NLS Framework for Teaching, and some non-fiction writing has links to other curricular areas e.g. an IT or history topic from the same, or earlier, term. Traditional tales are used as these provide a well-known basis that allows the children to focus on the writing process rather than be diverted by unfamiliar or challenging content.

# Planning grid

To aid planning, this grid refers to word, sentence and text level teaching objectives in the NLS framework for teaching.

## Term 1

| Word level | Page | Sentence level | Page | Text level | Page |
|---|---|---|---|---|---|
| 9 | 1 | 2 | 16, 17, 20, 21 | 6 | 1, 2 |
| | | 3 | 16, 17, 20, 21 | 7 | 5 |
| | | 5 | 2 | 8 | 3, 4 |
| | | | | 9 | 6, 7 |
| | | | | 10 | 8, 9, 10 |
| | | | | 14 | 11, 12, 13, 14, 15 |
| | | | | 15 | 16, 17 |
| | | | | 16 | 16, 17 |
| | | | | 17 | 18, 19, 20, 21 |

## Term 2

| Word level | Page | Sentence level | Page | Text level | Page |
|---|---|---|---|---|---|
| 7 | 24, 25 | | | 10 | 22, 23, 24, 25, 26, 27, 28, 29 |
| 8 | 37, 38, 40 | | | 11 | 30, 31 |
| | | | | 14 | 32, 33, 34 |
| | | | | 18 | 35, 36, 37, 38, 41 |
| | | | | 19 | 39, 40 |

## Term 3

| Word level | Page | Sentence level | Page | Text level | Page |
|---|---|---|---|---|---|
| | | 1 | 50, 51, 52, 53, 54, 55, 56, 57, 58, 59, 60, 61 | 7 | 45, 46, 47 |
| | | 3 | 50, 51 | 9 | 42, 43, 44 |
| | | | | 10 | 42, 43, 44 |
| | | | | 12 | 45, 46, 47 |
| | | | | 13 | 48, 49 |
| | | | | 20 | 50, 51, 52, 57, 58, 59, 60, 61 |
| | | | | 22 | 52, 53, 54, 55, 56, 57, 58, 59, 60, 61 |

## Term 1 Fiction

**Retelling a story**
**Main focus** Model text
**NLS teaching objectives** W9, T6

Blondie was zooming down the street on her micro scooter when she noticed the blue front door of the end house was wide open. She whizzed up the front path and threw her scooter to the ground. 'Hello!' she called loudly through the doorway. 'Hello?' There was no answer.

Blondie stepped into the narrow hall and looked into the kitchen. Her eyes widened as she saw a steaming plate of beef burgers. She bit into the first one. 'Yuk, onions!' she said and spat it out. She bit into the second one. 'Yuk, gherkins!' she said and spat it out. She bit into the last one. 'Mmmm,' she said, 'that's just right,' and she ate it all up.

Next Blondie went into the living room. She saw a CD player . . .

### Activities

- Use as a model to demonstrate how to retell a traditional tale (i.e. Goldilocks) as a modern version. Focus on the contemporary references in the story.
- Discuss words that have been introduced into the English language during the last 100 years.
- Discuss what could happen next.

- Continue this modern version of Goldilocks.

**Term 1 Fiction**

**Retelling a story**
**Main focus** Two narrators
**NLS teaching objectives** S5, T6

Mum always makes us beef burgers for tea on Mondays. Dad has gherkin in his, Mum has onion, but I just have mine plain. She had just put them on the table when we got an urgent call from Gran up the road. 'You've got to come round straight away!' she bellowed down the phone, 'the budgie has escaped.' I have to say that Gran's budgie is always escaping but we all ran off up the road. Mum reckoned the beef burgers would be OK for a while so we left them on the table.

The blonde-haired girl was just doing a third lap of honour on her new micro scooter when she noticed the front door of the end house was wide open. There was the most wonderful smell coming from inside. Almost without thinking, she left her scooter on the path and followed the aroma of freshly cooked beef burgers. It led her to the kitchen and there, on the table, were three delicious-looking beef burgers.

## Activities

- Use as a model to demonstrate how to tell a story using two narrators.
- Focus on the change from first to third person.
- Discuss how the story might continue, perhaps alternating between the two narrators.
- Focus on the use of a range of sentence types (i.e. simple, compound and complex) and the way this adds variety and pace to the story.

- Continue this modern version of Goldilocks using two narrators.

# Term 1 Fiction

**Summarising a story**
**Main focus** Using a limited number of words
(story pyramid) (see also page 4)
**NLS teaching objective** T8

1. Goldilocks

2. Cheeky, sneaky

3. Three bears' cottage

4. Things eaten and broken

5. Goldilocks eats the bears' porridge

6. Goldilocks breaks baby bear's little chair

7. Goldilocks falls asleep in baby bear's bed

8. The bears come home and Goldilocks runs away

Write:
1. the name of the main character
2. two words describing the main character
3. three words describing the setting
4. four words stating the story problem
5. five words describing the first event
6. six words describing the second event
7. seven words describing the third event
8. eight words describing the solution to the problem

## Activity

 • Use as a model to demonstrate how to summarise a known story in a limited number of words.

# Term 1
# Fiction

**Summarising a story** Story pyramid
**Main focus** Making notes
**NLS teaching objective** T8

1.\_\_\_\_

2.\_\_\_\_ \_\_\_\_

3.\_\_\_\_ \_\_\_\_ \_\_\_\_

4.\_\_\_\_ \_\_\_\_ \_\_\_\_ \_\_\_\_

5.\_\_\_\_ \_\_\_\_ \_\_\_\_ \_\_\_\_ \_\_\_\_

6.\_\_\_\_ \_\_\_\_ \_\_\_\_ \_\_\_\_ \_\_\_\_ \_\_\_\_

7. \_\_\_\_ \_\_\_\_ \_\_\_\_ \_\_\_\_ \_\_\_\_ \_\_\_\_ \_\_\_\_

8.\_\_\_\_ \_\_\_\_ \_\_\_\_ \_\_\_\_ \_\_\_\_ \_\_\_\_ \_\_\_\_ \_\_\_\_

Write:
1. the name of the main character
2. two words describing the main character
3. three words describing the setting
4. four words stating the story problem
5. five words describing the first event
6. six words describing the second event
7. seven words describing the third event
8. eight words describing the solution to the problem

## Activities

 • Use the story pyramid to demonstrate how to summarise a story in a limited number of words.

 • Use the story pyramid to summarise a story in a limited number of words.

## Term 1 Fiction

**Story planning** Planning frame
**Main focus** Making notes
**NLS teaching objective** T7

**Setting**

**Character**

**Theme**

**Orientation**

**Plot**

**Complication**

**Resolution/reorientation**

### Activities

- Use the planning frame to demonstrate how to make notes for a story.

- Use the planning frame to make own notes for a story.

# Term 1 Fiction

**Playscript**
**Main focus** Drafting (see also page 7)
**NLS teaching objective** T9

*Cast*
Alice
Alice's sister
White Rabbit
Narrator

*White Rabbit* (*breathlessly*): Oh dear! Oh dear! I shall be too late!
*Alice:* How curious.
*Narrator:* Alice followed the White Rabbit and found herself falling. She
    fell for what seemed like a very long time. She finally landed on a
    pile of dry leaves.
*Alice* (*amazed*): I don't seem to have hurt myself one bit. Oh, there's
    the White Rabbit! I can just see him down that passage.
*White Rabbit* (*from off-stage*): Oh, my ears and whiskers, how late it's
    getting!

## Activities

- Use to demonstrate how to turn part of a story (in this case the opening of
  *Alice in Wonderland*) into a playscript. Focus on the use of the narrator to
  move the story on.
- Discuss any changes or additions that would be needed to add clarity and
  detail.
- Add stage directions to the draft.

- Continue turning the story into a playscript.

**Term 1 Fiction**

**Playscripts**
**Main focus** Model text (see also page 6)
**NLS teaching objective** T9

*Characters*
Alice
Alice's sister
White Rabbit

*Alice and her sister are sitting in the sunshine on a grassy bank. Alice's sister is reading.*
*Alice is looking bored and restless.*
*Suddenly a White Rabbit rushes past Alice.*

*White Rabbit (breathlessly):* Oh dear! Oh dear! I shall be too late!
*He takes a watch from his waistcoat pocket, looks at it and rushes off.*
*Alice:* How curious.
*Alice jumps to her feet and follows the White Rabbit. They both disappear through the back of the stage. The stage lights dim until there is just one spotlight on a pile of leaves.*
Narrator: Alice followed the White Rabbit and found herself falling. She fell for what seemed like a very long time. She finally landed on a pile of dry leaves.
*Alice jumps from the darkness on to the spot-lit leaves.*
*Alice (amazed):* I don't seem to have hurt myself one bit. Oh, there's the White Rabbit! I can just see him down that passage.
*Alice runs off.*
*White Rabbit (from off-stage):* Oh, my ears and whiskers, how late it's getting!

## Activities

- Use as a model to demonstrate how to turn part of a story (in this case the opening of *Alice in Wonderland*) into a playscript.
- Demonstrate how to improve the draft version on page 6.
- Discuss how Alice's fall down the rabbit hole could be shown on stage.
- Explore how to add detail and move the story on by using a narrator and including stage directions.

- Continue turning the story of *Alice in Wonderland* into a playscript.

# Term 1 Poetry

**Personification**
**Main focus** Drafting (see also pages 9 and 10)
**NLS teaching objective** T10

*The Wind*

The wind walks around my house
Like a cat
Mewing and swishing
Its long tail.

The wind runs around my house
Like a panther
Rumbling and roaring
Knocking at the windows.

The wind stalks around my house
Like a lion
Roaring and growling
Waving the trees.

## Activities

- Use as a model to demonstrate how to write a draft version of a poem that involves personification.
- Focus on the second line in each verse and discuss what detail could be added to make the poem more effective (see page 9).
- Focus on the verbs and discuss alternatives.

- Add further verses to the poem.
- Improve the existing verses.

# Term 1 Poetry

**Personification**
**Main focus** Model text (see also pages 8 and 10)
**NLS teaching objective** T10

*The Wind*

The wind padding around my house
Is a cat on velvet paws
Mewing and purring,
Stroking the roof.

The wind prowling around my house
Is a panther with careful tread
Rumbling and grumbling,
Rattling the windows.

The wind stalking around my house
Is a lion after its prey
Roaring and growling,
Shaking the walls.

## Activities

 • Use to demonstrate how to improve a draft poem (see page 8). Focus on the improvements made in personification.

 • Continue the poem.

## Term 1 Poetry

**Personification**
**Main focus** Annotated model text (see also pages 8 and 9)
**NLS teaching objective** T10

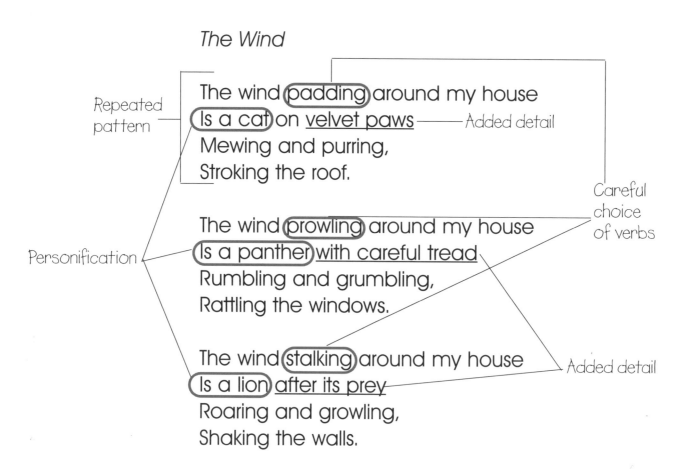

*The Wind*

Repeated pattern

The wind (padding) around my house
(Is a cat) on <u>velvet paws</u> —— Added detail
Mewing and purring,
Stroking the roof.

Personification

The wind (prowling) around my house
(Is a panther) <u>with careful tread</u>
Rumbling and grumbling,
Rattling the windows.

Careful choice of verbs

The wind (stalking) around my house
(Is a lion) <u>after its prey</u>
Roaring and growling,
Shaking the walls.

Added detail

### Activity

- Use as a model text to help the children identify the points raised on page 9.

## Term 1
## Non-fiction

**Biography** Planning frame
**Main focus** Making notes (see also page 12)
**NLS teaching objective** T14

## Subject

## Place and date of birth

## Early life

## Major events in life

## Place and date of death

### Activities

 • Use the planning frame to demonstrate how to make notes for a biography.

 • Use the planning frame to make own notes for a biography.

**Biography**
**Main focus** Planning (see also pages 11 and 13)
**NLS teaching objective** T14

## Subject
Guy Fawkes

## Place and date of birth
York, 13 April (?) 1570

## Early life
Educated in York
Influenced by Roman Catholics
1593 joined Spanish army
Wounded twice and became expert in mining and use of gunpowder
Brave
Converted to Catholicism

## Major events in life
Involved in plot to blow up House of Lords, killing members of Parliament and King
King alerted to the plot
Early hours of 5 Nov 1605 Guy Fawkes discovered during a search of cellars along with gunpowder, wood, coal and food
Tortured to reveal the names of the rest of the plotters

## Place and date of death
Hanged in London on 31 Jan 1606

### Activities

• Use as a model to demonstrate how to plan a biography.

• Add further information after doing some more research.

**Term 1
Non-fiction**

**Biography**
**Main focus** Model draft (see also pages 11 and 12)
**NLS teaching objective** T14

## The life of Guy Fawkes

Guy Fawkes was born in York. His date of birth is thought to have been around 13 April 1570.

Fawkes was educated in York and was influenced by Roman Catholics at school. In 1593, he joined the Spanish army. Guy Fawkes was wounded twice and became an expert in mining and in the use of gunpowder. He was said to have been a very brave man. At some time in his life, he converted to Catholicism.

Because of his expertise with explosives, Guy Fawkes was asked to become involved in a Catholic plot to blow up the House of Lords. The plotters hoped this would involve killing many members of Parliament and the Protestant King.

King James I was alerted to the plot because an anonymous letter was sent to a member of the government. In the early hours of 5 November 1605, the King organised a search of the cellars beneath the House of Lords. Guy Fawkes was discovered, along with gunpowder, wood, coal and food.

It is thought he was severely tortured so that he revealed the names of the rest of the plotters.

Guy Fawkes was hanged in London on 31 January 1606.

**Activities**

- Use to demonstrate how to turn a plan (see page 12) into a draft biography. Add any further information.

- Focus on the use of the past tense. Discuss what time markers are used (e.g. dates).

# Term 1
## Non-fiction

**Autobiography**
**Main focus** Writing with brevity
**NLS teaching objective** T14

---

## Lonely guy looking for friends

I enjoy planning and plotting. I like to organise events that go with a bang. People say I am brave and cheerful. I think I'm easy to get on with. Please contact me before 5 November as I may be busy after that date.

---

### Activities

- Demonstrate how to write a brief synopsis of a subject's personality.
- Write responses to the advert.

- Write other lonely hearts adverts for famous people or characters from books.

## Term 1
## Non-fiction

**Autobiography**
**Main focus** Writing concisely
**NLS teaching objective** T14

The Cellar
Under the House of Lords
London

5 November

Dear sir

I would like to apply for the job, in your fast-food restaurant, that was advertised in the *Daily Fryer* last week.

I was educated in York and have recently left the army. Whilst serving in the armed forces, I specialised in mining and explosives. I now find myself without employment due to a recent project that did not go quite the way I intended.

I am hard-working and I get on well with people. I can work as part of a team or independently. I can use my initiative and don't crack easily under pressure.

I look forward to hearing from you soon.

Yours faithfully

*Guy Fawkes*

Guy Fawkes

### Activities

- Use as a model to demonstrate how to write concisely, covering the salient points.

- Write letters applying for jobs on behalf of other historical or book characters.

## Term 1
### Non-fiction

**Newspapers**
**Main focus** Writing in a journalistic style (see also page 17)
**NLS teaching objectives** S2, S3, T15, T16

# Gunpowder plot foiled at eleventh hour

**A man was arrested in the early hours of this morning in connection with a suspected attempt on the lives of the Government and the King.**

Guy Fawkes, 36, originally of York, was found lurking in the cellars beneath the House of Lords. Also found in the cellars were quantities of gunpowder hidden beneath piles of wood and coal along with a substantial supply of food. Officers who searched Mr Fawkes said he was carrying several packs of matches.

Officers questioned by our reporters revealed they had been asked to search the cellars by none other than the King himself. 'He said something about a letter having been received,' one officer told us.

Fawkes has been taken to the Tower of London to await trial. He will be questioned further today in an attempt to gain information about other members of the gunpowder plot gang.

## Activities

- Use as a model to demonstrate how to write a newspaper article.
- Discuss the journalisitic style and tone. Focus on the headline.
- Discuss whether the article is balanced or biased.
- Focus on the use of the passive voice. Discuss the effect this has on a reader.

- Think of a different headline that summarises the article.
- Continue the article.
- Write a newspaper article about Guy Fawkes's execution.

**Term 1**
**Non-fiction**

**Newspapers**
**Main focus** Writing in a journalistic style (see also page 16)
**NLS teaching objectives** S2, S3, T15, T16

# Gunpowder plot foiled at eleventh hour

Headline

Introduction gives overview

When

**A man was arrested in (the early hours of this morning) in connection with a suspected attempt on the lives of the Government and the King.**

Who

Where

Past tense

Guy Fawkes, 36, originally of York, was found lurking in the cellars beneath the House of Lords. Also found in the cellars were quantities of gunpowder hidden beneath piles of wood and coal along with a substantial supply of food. Officers who searched Mr Fawkes said he was carrying several packs of matches. Past tense

Officers questioned by our reporters revealed they had been asked to search the cellars by none other than the King himself. 'He said something about a letter having been received,' one officer told us.

Fawkes has been taken to the Tower of London to await trial. He will be questioned further today in an attempt to gain information about other members of the gunpowder plot gang.

Passive voice, concealed agent

**Activity**

• Use as a model text to help the children identify the points raised on page 16.

## Term 1
## Non-fiction

**Historical reports** Planning frame
**Main focus** Making notes for a non-chronological report
(see also page 19)
**NLS teaching objective** T17

**Place**


**Where it is**


**Brief history**


**What it was used for**


**What it is used for now**


**Interesting facts**

 • Use the planning frame to demostrate how to make notes for a historical report.

 • Use the planning frame to demostrate how to make own notes for a historical report.

# Term 1
## Non-fiction

**Historical reports**
**Main focus** Planning a non-chronological report (see also page 18)
**NLS teaching objective** T17

# The Tower of London

**Place**
The Tower of London

**Where it is**
Tower Hill, London

**Brief history**
Built during reign of King Harold
Started as simple earth-and-timber fortress in 1067
1078 work started, on same site, on second fortress. Built of stone – known as White Tower. Finished in 1097
Over next 200 years, fortress was expanded until it covered 18 acres of land. Had 20 towers

**What it was used for**
Used for many things including home to Kings and Queens, the Royal Mint and a zoo
Known mainly in the past as a prison
Traitors to the Crown imprisoned and heads chopped off/or were hanged
Only nobility executed at the Tower
Public executions carried out on Tower Hill, watched by 100s of people
Late 19C Tower in no state to house prisoners
Repaired due to interest by Queen Victoria's husband. Became a tourist attraction

**What it is used for now**
Tourist attraction – $2\frac{1}{2}$ million visitors/year
Houses Crown Jewels – have actually been kept there since 14C, moved to secret location during 2nd WW
Ravens legend – if they leave Tower the White Tower will crumble and England will suffer great disaster
Protected by Royal decree. Cared for by Raven Master
Only time no ravens recorded – 1946, just after 2nd WW
Beefeaters – Yeoman Warders used to guard prisoners. Now responsible for security and take tourists on guided tours
All ex-members of armed forces

**Interesting facts**
Most recent prisoners kept in Tower during 1st and 2nd World Wars
Rudolf Hess, deputy führer of Nazi Germany, last prisoner held in Tower, May 17-21 1941

## Activity

- Use to demonstrate how to plan a historical report. Focus on organising facts under relevant headings (see also pages 20 and 21).

# Term 1
## Non-fiction

**Historical reports**
**Main focus** Drafting a non-chronological report (see also page 21)
**NLS teaching objectives** S2, S3, T17

## The Tower of London

The Tower of London is situated on Tower Hill in London, England.

It was built during the reign of King Harold. It started as a simple earth-and-timber fortress in 1067 and 200 years later covered 18 acres of land and had 20 towers. The Tower takes its name from the White Tower which was built in 1097.

The Tower of London has been used for many things including the main residence of Kings and Queens, the Royal Mint, even a zoo. However, it is known mainly as having been used as a prison in the past. Famous prisoners were Guy Fawkes and a number of Henry VIII's wives.

The Tower was used to house traitors to the Crown and they invariably had their heads chopped off or were hanged. Only nobility were executed at the Tower. Public executions were carried out on Tower Hill and were usually watched by many hundreds of people.

By the late 19th century the Tower had fallen into disrepair. It was renovated because Prince Albert, Queen Victoria's husband, became interested in the building and its history.

Nowadays, the Tower is one of London's main tourist attractions. Over 2½ million visitors come to the Tower every year. The Crown Jewels can be seen at the Tower. They have been housed there since the 14th century but were taken to a secret location during the Second World War. The 'Beefeaters' or Yeoman Warders are something else that tourists come to see. They used to guard prisoners in the Tower but now they are responsible for security and taking tourists on guided tours. Yeoman Warders are all ex-servicemen.

## Activities

- Use as a model to demonstrate how to turn a plan into a draft report.

- Focus on the mix of past and present tense, the use of technical vocabulary and the use of the passive voice to add to the impersonal style (see also pages 19 and 21).

## Term 1
## Non-fiction

**Historical reports**
**Main focus** Drafting a non-chronological report (see also page 20)
**NLS teaching objectives** S2, S3, T17

# The Tower of London

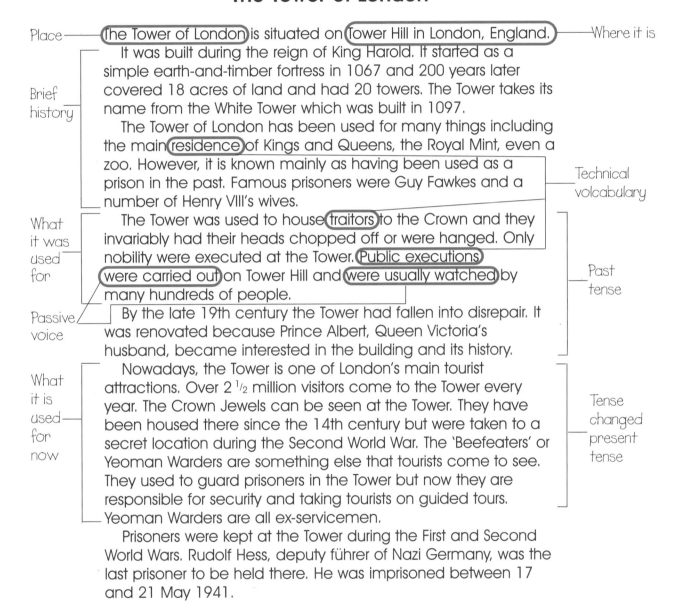

Place — The Tower of London is situated on Tower Hill in London, England. — Where it is

Brief history — It was built during the reign of King Harold. It started as a simple earth-and-timber fortress in 1067 and 200 years later covered 18 acres of land and had 20 towers. The Tower takes its name from the White Tower which was built in 1097.

The Tower of London has been used for many things including the main residence of Kings and Queens, the Royal Mint, even a zoo. However, it is known mainly as having been used as a prison in the past. Famous prisoners were Guy Fawkes and a number of Henry VIII's wives. — Technical vocabulary

What it was used for — The Tower was used to house traitors to the Crown and they invariably had their heads chopped off or were hanged. Only nobility were executed at the Tower. Public executions were carried out on Tower Hill and were usually watched by many hundreds of people. — Past tense

Passive voice — By the late 19th century the Tower had fallen into disrepair. It was renovated because Prince Albert, Queen Victoria's husband, became interested in the building and its history.

What it is used for now — Nowadays, the Tower is one of London's main tourist attractions. Over 2 ½ million visitors come to the Tower every year. The Crown Jewels can be seen at the Tower. They have been housed there since the 14th century but were taken to a secret location during the Second World War. The 'Beefeaters' or Yeoman Warders are something else that tourists come to see. They used to guard prisoners in the Tower but now they are responsible for security and taking tourists on guided tours. Yeoman Warders are all ex-servicemen. — Tense changed present tense

Prisoners were kept at the Tower during the First and Second World Wars. Rudolf Hess, deputy führer of Nazi Germany, was the last prisoner to be held there. He was imprisoned between 17 and 21 May 1941.

## Activity

- Use as a model text to help the children identify the points raised on page 20.

**Term 2 Fiction**

**Mystery stories**
**Main focus** Model text (see also page 23)
**NLS teaching objective** T10

When Ginny returned to the cottage, there was no trace of anything unusual. Mrs Downs was calmly pottering in the garden with her secateurs in hand, snipping gently at the dead heads of her dahlias. Ginny called out to her as she slowed her bike at the gate, asking if the strange, angry boy had visited again.

"Strange boy?" queried Mrs·Downs. "No, love, no one's been for a couple of days, except for you."

Not again, thought Ginny with a rising sense of panic. She had clearly seen the boy arguing with Mrs Downs yesterday, and Mrs Downs knew it. Yet here she was, denying it completely, and acting like all the others. Why was everyone pretending this boy didn't exist?

**Activities**

- Use to identify the key features of a mystery. Focus on the question at the end of the passage. Discuss possible answers.
- Discuss the vocabulary that indicates this is part of a mystery.

- Describe a scene that could precede the passage.
- Write a further episode.

## Term 2 Fiction

**Mystery stories**
**Main focus** Annotated model text (see also page 22)
**NLS teaching objective** T10

When Ginny returned to the cottage, there was

Implies there should be — no trace of anything unusual. Mrs Downs was calmly — Implies calm state is strange

pottering in the garden with her secateurs in hand,

snipping gently at the dead heads of her dahlias.

Ginny called out to her as she slowed her bike at the

gate, asking if the strange, angry boy had visited again. — Sense of mystery

    "Strange boy?" queried Mrs Downs. "No, love, no

one's been for a couple of days, except for you."

    Not again, thought Ginny with a rising sense of panic. — Indicator of a problem

She had clearly seen the boy arguing with Mrs Downs

yesterday, and Mrs Downs knew it. Yet here she was, — Sense of mystery

denying it completely, and acting  like all the others.

Why was everyone pretending this boy didn't — Feeling of conspiracy

exist?

Sense of mystery

## Activity

- Use as a model text to help the children identify the points raised on page 22.

## Term 2 Fiction

**Historical stories**
**Main focus** Model text (see also page 25)
**NLS teaching objectives** W7, T10

With Father away, the house was very different. Mother spent most of her time in her room with The Vapours. Emilia wasn't sure what The Vapours was, but Cook kept the children away from Mother's room, and told them to keep quiet in that wing of the house. Now no one watched over them, and they wandered the house and the grounds at liberty. Only Cook and Tilly, the kitchen maid, remained, both too busy to look after children. Cook kept sighing heavily and asking what would become of them all.

"'Twas a bad day, a fearsome bad day," she kept repeating.

### Activities

- Focus on the key features and vocabulary that indicate this is an episode from a story from the past.
- Discuss the names of the characters, Emilia, Mother, Father, Cook, Tilly.
- Compare how the vocabulary would change if told in the present.
- Brainstorm possible characters for the story.

- Write an episode in which Cook leaves, telling what Mother does, or what Emilia does, to help Tilly to look after them all.

# Term 2 Fiction

**Historical stories**
**Main focus** Annotated model text (see also page 24)
**NLS teaching objectives** W7, T10

*Formal useage*

With (Father) away, the house was very different.

(Mother) spent most of her time in her room with

*Not current term*

The Vapours. Emilia wasn't sure what (The Vapours)

*Indicates society of the past*

was, but (Cook) kept the children away from

Mother's room, and told them to keep quiet in

that wing of the house. Now no one watched

over them, and they wandered the house and

*Old fashioned name*

the grounds at liberty. Only Cook and (Tilly,) the

*Rare in modern setting*

(kitchen maid,) remained, both too busy to look

after children. Cook kept sighing heavily and

asking what would become of them all.

("Twas) a bad day, a (fearsome bad) day," she

kept repeating.

*Old fashioned language*

## Activity

- Use as a model text to help the children identify the points raised on page 24.

**Term 2 Fiction**

**Fantasy stories**
**Main focus** Model text (see also page 27)
**NLS teaching objective** T10

The silver moon gleamed upon the winged horse as it stopped to drink from the pool. Jamie kept still, scarcely daring to breathe. As he watched, three more flew down to the glade. Sitting on their backs were the gremlins, just as the old wizard had described. Their gnarled faces were twisted with glee as they threw long silver chains over the drinking horse. It immediately knelt in surrender, and another gremlin scrambled up out of the undergrowth to mount the tamed horse. With a swoosh of beating wings, the horses rose from the pool and soared into the night.

## Activities

- Discuss the vocabulary that shows this is a fantasy. Compare with other fantasy stories.
- Add other characters based on the passage.

- Add a further episode.
- List characters that could be written into a fantasy.
- Write a character sketch of a gremlin.

**Term 2 Fiction**

**Fantasy stories**
**Main focus** Annotated model text (see also page 26)
**NLS teaching objective** T10

The silver moon gleamed upon the winged horse as it stopped to drink from the pool. Jamie kept still, scarcely daring to breathe. As he watched, three more flew down to the glade. Sitting on their backs were the gremlins, just as the old wizard had described. Their gnarled faces were twisted with glee as they threw long silver chains over the drinking horse. It immediately knelt in surrender, and another gremlin scrambled up out of the undergrowth to mount the tamed horse. With a swoosh of beating wings, the horses rose from the pool and soared into the night.

Fantasy creature = clear indicator of genre

Standard fantasy character

Unusual image

Unusual image

**Activity**

- Use as a model to help the children identify the points raised on page 26.

**Term 2 Fiction**

**Science fiction stories**
**Main focus** Model text (see also page 29)
**NLS teaching objective** T10

The Varja faced the Krildar over the wide stretch of the salt bed. The three moons of Varj cast a clear light in the thin atmosphere, showing the Krildar hordes as they hovered in their ships above the precious red salt. Though the Varja were outnumbered, they were ready to fight to the death. If the red salt was captured, they would become slaves, transported to Krildon, while their home planet was mined and stripped of all its valuable resources.

### Activities

- Discuss how the choice of vocabulary indicates genre. Focus on invented words and features that are obviously not of the earth.
- Brainstorm stock characters and settings.
- Draw comparisons with other science fiction stories.

- Describe a setting that could be used for science fiction.
- Change a common setting into a sci-fi setting.

# Term 2 Fiction

**Science fiction stories**
**Main focus** Annotated model text (see also page 28)
**NLS teaching objective** T10

The (Varja) faced the (Krildar) over the wide stretch of the salt bed. The (three) moons of (Vari) cast a clear light in the thin atmosphere, showing the Krildar hordes as they hovered in their ships above the precious (red salt.) Though the Varja were outnumbered, they were ready to fight to the death. If the red salt was captured, they would become slaves, transported to (Krildon,) while their (home planet) was mined and stripped of all its valuable resources.

*Invented use of people/place*

*Strong invented names*

*3 moons = clear indicator of genre*

*Abnormal colour adjective*

*Invented use of people/ place*

*Invented name*

*Clear indicator of genre*

**Activity**

- Use as a model text to help the children identify the points raised on page 28.

## Term 2 Fiction

**Passage of time**
**Main focus** Model text using flash-back technique
(see also page 31)
**NLS teaching objective** T11

Bill sat and watched the group playing roller-hockey. Their voices faded as his chin dropped forward on to his chest in the warm sun.

"To you, Bill! To you!" The heavy wet football arched in the air above him. Now was his chance to score and win the match. He kept his eyes focused on the ball as his feet struggled to gain a grip in the mud, ready to leap up and head the ball straight into goal. Smack! Right on to his forehead went the wet leather and suddenly he was face down in the stinking mud.

"Are you all right? Are you hurt?" came the voices of boys bending over him. He slowly opened his eyes and saw the boys in their roller-hockey helmets gathered round in concern. To think he still dwelt on that missed goal, all these years later!

### Activities

- Discuss how the reader knows which part is from a past time, and how it returns to the present.
- Discuss how the past can be described in stories through devices other than dreams.

- Draft a story with a dream sequence, taking a character back or forward in time.

**Term 2 Fiction**

**Passage of time**
**Main focus** Annotated model text (see also page 30)
**NLS teaching objective** T11

Bill sat and watched the group playing (roller-hockey.) — Modern reference

Their (voices faded as his chin dropped forward on to) (his chest) in the warm sun. — Implies sleep

Flashback sequence in a dream —

"To you, Bill! To you!" The (heavy wet football) arched in the air above him. Now was his chance to score and win the match. He kept his eyes focused on the ball as his feet struggled to gain a grip in the mud, ready to leap up and head the ball straight into goal. Smack! Right on to his forehead went the (wet leather) and suddenly he was face down in the stinking mud.

Reference to past-times —

"Are you all right? Are you hurt?" (came the voices) of boys bending over him. (He slowly opened his eyes) and saw the boys in their (roller-hockey) helmets gathered round in concern. To think he still dwelt on that missed goal, all these years later!

Dream of past or happening in the present?

Woke

Back to present

**Activity**

 • Use as a model text to help the children identify the points raised on page 30.

# Term 2 Fiction

**Commentaries**
**Main focus** Planning (see also pages 33 and 34)
**NLS teaching objective** T14

| Features | Comments |
|---|---|
| *Setting*<br>Cottage in a wood | This is a typical fairy-story setting |
| *Characters*<br>3 bears and Goldilocks, a child | Goldilocks has bad manners, she should not go in houses uninvited and eat their food, and break things. She deserved to be frightened by the bears |
| *Plot*<br>3 bears want to eat their breakfast. They go for a walk while it cools | Unrealistic fantasy which is OK for a fairy tale. |
| *Complication*<br>Goldilocks is hungry and tries their breakfasts | The original author must have wanted this to be a cautionary tale. Goldilocks was inconsiderate and was frightened as a result |
| *Theme*<br>Bears and children don't mix | The theme is vague. Goldilocks is the central character, but she is the one in the wrong. Fairy tales usually have a good main character |
| *Genre and language features*<br>Fairy tale<br>Rule of 3 | Uses the rule of 3 to good effect – 3 bears, 3 episodes (porridge, chairs, beds) |
| *Summary* | |

## Activity

- Use as a model to structure a commentary on an author's work.

|  |  |
|---|---|
| *Plot* |  |
| *Complication* |  |
| *Theme* |  |
| *Genre and language features* |  |

## Activities

- Use the planning frame to demonstrate how to structure a commentary on an author's work.

- Use the planning frame to make own notes for a commentary.

**Term 2 Fiction**

**Commentaries**
**Main focus** Model text (see also page 33)
**NLS teaching objective** T14

## Goldilocks and the Three Bears

This story is a traditional story set in a cottage in a forest. Although it is described as a fairy tale, the element of magic is missing. Instead it is more of a cautionary tale.

The author might have wanted the story to teach a lesson to readers. It is easy to read and to remember, because the author uses the rule of three. There are three bears, followed by three episodes when Goldilocks tries first the porridge, second the chairs and, lastly, the beds. Repeating episodes and characters three times makes this easy to remember.

**Activity**

- Draw attention to use of connectives to structure commentaries and the giving of evidence from the text to support opinions.

## Term 2
## Non-fiction

**Discussion text**
**Main focus** Brainstorming (see also pages 36 and 37)
**NLS teaching objective** T18

**Issue**: Playing outdoor sports in winter

| **Points for** | **Points against** |
|---|---|
| Healthy exercise | Cold |
| Burns off energy | Wet |
| Fresh air | Chapped lips/knees etc |
| | Might catch pneumonia |

| **Emotive/persuasive evidence for** | **Emotive/persuasive evidence against** |
|---|---|
| Dinner, then a game of football in the wind woke me up and gave me energy | I got wet and muddy, and my mum had to wash all my clothes |

### Activities

- Use as a starting point to add opinions and supporting evidence about an issue.

- Use the planning frame on page 36 to structure points for an argument or discussion.

**Term 2**
**Non-fiction**

**Discussion text**
**Main focus** Making notes (see also page 41)
**NLS teaching objective** T18

| Issue | |
|---|---|
| **Points for** | **Points against** |
| **Emotive/persuasive evidence for** | **Emotive/persuasive evidence against** |

**Activities**

- Use as a planning frame to demonstrate how to construct an effective argument.

- Use the planning frame to make own notes to construct an effective argument.

# Term 2
## Non-fiction

**Discussion text**
**Main focus** Annotated model text (see also pages 36 and 38)
**NLS teaching objectives** W8, T18

I believe that forcing children to play sports during the winter months is a bad thing and should be stopped.

Children should be kept warm during the winter months or they may catch colds, flu or more serious illnesses like pneumonia

Often the weather is extremely bad. It frequently rains, hails or snows, the ground is hard and frozen, and the wind is bitterly cold.

Children huddle together to keep warm while the game gets organised by the teacher, which makes their muscles cold. Then they are expected to run around without having warmed up first. This can result in strained or even torn muscles.

Learning skills in these conditions is often impossible. It is difficult to hear the teacher's instructions when the wind is howling, or your teeth are chattering loudly.

It has been argued that outdoor sport is healthy and gives us energy. This may be a valid point, but I would suggest that this could take place indoors just as effectively.

I played football last week when it had been raining hard. The ground was heavy and muddy. It was difficult to run or kick the ball, so I got little exercise. All I got was cold and dirty. However, I played badminton at the sports centre after school. It was warm and dry, and I got far more benefit from that than the outdoor sport.

In conclusion, I believe that this practice, of forcing children out into freezing conditions, is cruel and without any obvious benefit.

I appeal to all pupils to do something about this. I urge you to bring letters from home to complain about this. If we act together, we can make a difference.

## Activities

- Used to demonstrate how to convert notes into a logical sequence to support a point of view.

- Write an argument from an opposing point of view using this as a model.

# Term 2
## Non-fiction

**Discussion text**
**Main focus** Annotated model text (see also page 36 and 37)
**NLS teaching objectives** W8, T18

Opening statement of position — (I believe that) forcing children to play sports during the winter months is a bad thing and should be stopped.

Argument in support

Children should be kept warm during the winter months or (they may catch colds,) flu or more serious illnesses like pneumonia

Argument in support — (Often the weather is extremely bad.) It frequently rains, hails or snows, the ground is hard and frozen, and the wind is bitterly cold.

(Children huddle together to keep warm) while the game gets

Cause and effect volcabulary — organised by the teacher, (which makes) their muscles cold. (Then) they are expected to run around without having warmed up first. (This can result) in strained or even torn muscles.

Cause and effect volcabulary

Learning skills in these conditions is often impossible. It is difficult to hear the teacher's instructions when the wind is howling, or your teeth are chattering loudly.

It has been argued that outdoor sport is healthy and gives us energy. This may be a valid point, but I would suggest that this could take place indoors just as effectively.

Pre-empt counter arguments

Supporting evidence

(I played football last week when it had been raining hard.) The ground was heavy and muddy. It was difficult to run or kick the ball, so I got little exercise. All I got was cold and dirty. (However, I played badminton at the sports centre after school.) It was warm and dry, and I got far more benefit from that than the outdoor sport.

Persuasive example

Persuasive example

Closing statement repeats opening statement — (In conclusion,) I believe that this practice, of forcing children out into freezing conditions, is cruel and without any obvious benefit.

Call to action

(I appeal) to all pupils to do something about this. (I urge) you to bring letters from home to complain about this. (If we act together, we can make a difference.)

Call to action

Strong close

## Activity

- Use as a model text to help the children identify the points raised on page 37.

**Discussion text**
**Main focus** Planning (see also page 40)
**NLS teaching objective** T19

## Children using mobile phones

| Statement | Counter-statement |
|---|---|
| Mobile phones are part of everyday life | But they might damage health |
| Mobile phones may damage your health | But the claim is not proven |
| Children spend too much time sending text messages | But this is fun and an easy way to reach friends |
| Parents get pressured into buying the latest models for children | You can buy pay-as-u-go phones which keep the cost down and teach you to manage your money |
| Children should be allowed to use phones as much as they want | But they can be a nuisance, particularly in school |

Balance points to show counter argument

| Strong points | |
|---|---|
| | |

**Activities**

- Use as a stimulus to brainstorm claims and counter-claims in a balanced argument, identifying the strengths and weaknesses.

- Use as a planning frame to structure own balanced discussion text.

**Term 2**
**Non-fiction**

**Discussion text**
**Main focus** Model text (see also page 39)
**NLS teaching objectives** W8, T19

Mobile phones have become a part of everyday life. However, concern has been expressed over some issues involved in their use by children.

Many teachers believe mobile phones are a nuisance in school, but they can be very useful to pupils. For example, if a parent were to be delayed in collecting his or her child, he or she could easily get a message to the child. This would mean the child would be safer than if the message hadn't been sent. Pupils and teachers should be able to decide a system of rules for their use in school.

Another issue is that of health. There have been reports they give out radiation, which may result in brain damage. However, these claims have little or no evidence to support them.

A further cause for concern is that pressure is put on parents to buy new and up-to-date models. Parents should be able to decide whether this is an issue for themselves. Furthermore, using a pay-as-you-go type of phone may be a good tool to teach children how to handle money.

In conclusion, although mobile phones are a useful tool for keeping in touch and are now a normal part of life, care should be taken that they are not overused or misused in school, where they would be seen as a nuisance instead of a helpful, essential item.

**Activity**

- Draw attention to using a balance of statements. Focus on the use of connectives and cause and effect vocabulary to give a sequence of arguments.

**Term 2**
**Non-fiction**

**Discussion text**
**Main focus** Making notes (see also page 35)
**NLS teaching objective** T18

**Statement of issue:**

Many people believe that . . .

However . . .

A further issue is . . .

Alternatively . . .

In conclusion . . .

**Activities**

- Use the planning frame to demonstrate how to make notes for a balanced piece of discursive writing.

- Use the planning frame to make own notes for a balanced piece of argumentative writing.

## Term 3 Fiction

**Blurbs**
**Main focus** Model text (see also page 43)
**NLS teaching objectives** T9, T10

## "Curiouser and curiouser!" cried Alice.

An ordinary river-outing leads an ordinary girl into an extraordinary sequence of events.
When Alice sees a white rabbit in a waistcoat, she follows him into a strange underground world, peopled with weird and wonderful characters.

Will Alice grow back to life-size? Can she keep her head on her shoulders? Will she ever find her way back to the riverbank?

A wonderful array of improbable events occurs when Alice's curiosity leads her into a wonderland of strange characters in this fantasy adventure for young children.

*"One of those rare books you'll enjoy again and again."*
**BOOK NEWS MONTHLY**
*"Enchantment for children of all ages."*
**CARROLL TIMES**

### Activities

- Draw attention to the short quotation to 'hook' the reader. Focus on brevity, and not telling the story but giving enough detail to entice the reader.

- Compare with books in the classroom to explore the layout and use of font.
- Write own blurb for favourite books.

**Term 3 Fiction**

**Blurbs**
**Main focus** Planning (see also page 42)
**NLS teaching objectives** T9, T10

## Headline: quotation

"Curiouser and curiouser!" cried Alice.

## A glimpse of the story in two sentences

An ordinary river-outing leads an ordinary girl into an extraordinary sequence of events.
When Alice sees a white rabbit in a waistcoat, she follows him into a strange underground world, peopled with weird and wonderful characters.

## Three rhetorical questions

Will Alice grow back to life-size? Can she keep her head on her shoulders? Will she ever find her way back to the riverbank?

## Summarising statement, including genre and setting

A wonderful array of improbable events occurs when Alice's curiosity leads her into a wonderland of strange characters in this fantasy adventure for young children.

## Review quotations

"One of those rare books you'll enjoy again and again."  BOOK NEWS MONTHLY
"Enchantment for children of all ages." CARROLL TIMES

### Activities

- Use this imaginary book blurb as a model for writing about the books you are reading.

- The planning frame (see page 44) can be used to support own book blurb.

## Term 3
## Fiction

**Blurbs** Planning frame
**Main focus** Making notes (see also page 43)
**NLS teaching objectives** T9, T10

| |
|---|
| **Headline: quotation** |
| **A glimpse of the story in two sentences** |
| **Three rhetorical questions** |
| **Summarising statement, including genre and setting** |
| **Review quotations** |

### Activities

 • Use the planning frame to demonstrate how to make notes for a blurb.

 • Use the planning frame to make own notes for a blurb.

## Term 3 Fiction

**Annotating a poem**
**Main focus** Marking text in response to questions (see also page 46)
**NLS teaching objectives** T7, T12

Speak roughly to your little boy,
And beat him when he sneezes;
He only does it to annoy,
Because he knows it teases.

I speak severely to my boy,
I beat him when he sneezes;
For he can thoroughly enjoy
The pepper when he pleases!

(from Lewis Carroll, 1832–1898)


Speak gently to the little child!
Its love be sure to gain;
Teach it in accents soft and mild:
It may not long remain.

Speak gently to the young, for they
Will have enough to bear –
Pass through this life as best they may,
'Tis full of anxious care!

(from David Bates, 1809–1870)

## Activities

- Use these two short extracts to demonstrate how to annotate a passage in response to questions (see page 46). Use half the prepared questions.

- The pupils should mark their own copies in response to the remaining questions.

# Term 3 Poetry

**Annotating a poem**
**Main focus** Questions for annotating the poems (see also page 45)
**NLS teaching objectives** T7, T12

1. One poem is a parody of the other. Identify which is which.
2. Circle the contrasting adverbs in each poem.
3. Are there any adjectives in these poems? Circle them.
4. Which two lines in the Lewis Carroll poem are meant to be a joke? Underline them.
5. Why does Lewis Carroll mention pepper?
6. Which verbs are used as a command? Circle them all.
7. What effect does the use of the command (imperative verb) have on the reader?
8. Which line tells the reader life for a Victorian child could be short? Circle it.
9. Which line tells the reader Victorian life was full of problems? Circle it.
10. Is there any vocabulary that shows these poems were written in the past? Circle any words or phrases.
11. Which author lived longest?

**Activity**

 • Use these questions as a starting point for annotating the text (see page 47).

## Term 3 Poetry

**Annotating a poem**
**Main focus** Model text (see also pages 45 and 46)
**NLS teaching objectives** T7, T12

PARODY

Command

Joke lines

Adverbs

Speak roughly to your little boy,
And beat him when he sneezes;
He only does it to annoy,
Because he knows it teases.

Adj.

I speak severely to my boy,
I beat him when he sneezes;
For he can thoroughly enjoy
The pepper when he pleases!

Cause and effect

(from Lewis Carroll, 1832–1898) — Longest lived

Command

ORIGINAL

Adverbs

Speak gently to the little child!
Its love be sure to gain;
Teach it in accents soft and mild:
It may not long remain.

Adjectives

Victorian life was short

Addresses the reader personally

Speak gently to the young, for they
Will have enough to bear –
Pass through this life as best they may,
'Tis full of anxious care!

Old fashioned vocabulary. Life full of problems

Adj.

(from David Bates, 1809-1870)

---

**Activity**

• Use as a model to help the children identify the points on page 46.

**Term 3
Poetry**

Sequence of poetry
**Main focus** Thematic links (see also page 49)
**NLS teaching objective** T13

*Colour Calendar*

*Spring*
Yellow buds the branch,
Bursts over the wakening earth,
Lightens the evening.

*Summer*
Green paints the meadow,
Colours oak and willow tree,
Holds up the flowers.

*Autumn*
Bronze brittles the leaf,
Blows gold, amber, emerald.
Jewel-bright firework.

*Winter*
White traces cobwebs
Dusts the hedge and house and street.
Pulls down the darkness.

## Activities

- Use as a model for writing a sequence of poems on a common theme or form.
- Draw attention to the theme of colour (or season).
- Revise personification from term 1.

- Use one of the senses as a theme for a haiku calendar (e.g. smell).

**Term 3 Poetry**

**Sequence of poetry**
**Main focus** Thematic links
**NLS teaching objective** T13

*Colour Calendar*

Repeated
pattern
common to
each haiku

Used as verbs

*Spring*
Yellow (buds) the branch,
(Bursts) over the wakening earth,
Lightens the evening.

Verb

*Summer*
Green (paints) the meadow,
Colours oak and willow tree,
Holds up the flowers.

Verb

*Autumn*
Bronze (brittles) the leaf,
Blows gold, amber, emerald.
Jewel-bright firework.
Imagery

Verb

*Winter*
White (traces) cobwebs
Dusts the hedge and house and street.
Pulls down the darkness.
Imagery

**Activity**

• Use as a model text to help the children identify the points on page 48.

49

**Term 3
Non-fiction**

**Visitors' guides
Main focus** Impersonal voice (Model text) (see also page 51)
**NLS teaching objectives** S1, S3, T20

## Ringlow Park Internet Gardens

When you enter Ringlow Park Gardens, the first area you come to is the Laptop Glade. This has been lavishly planted with laptops, palmtops and organisers, and is best seen in the spring.

The winding rustic path takes you past the mouse garden. Here, the area has been colonised by the intelli-mouse, completely overtaking the roller mice, who have moved to share the edges of the stream with fading mouse-mats.

The formal hardware gardens are a must for visitors in the autumn months. These hold the National Collection of printers, the grey shades of which are shown to best effect in the softer light of September and October. Arranged among the printers is an assortment of desktop PCs, fax machines and cables, while CD-ROMs reflect the light in a stunning end to the tour.

Souvenirs are available in the gift shop.

We hope you have enjoyed your visit, and look forward to welcoming you again.

### Activities

- Draw attention the fact that, although the content is fictional, this text uses the passive voice and present tense as in an authentic non-fiction text.

- Create a fantasy place and write a visitors' guide.

## Term 3
### Non-fiction

**Visitors' guides**
**Main Focus** Impersonal voice (model text) (see also page 50)
**NLS teaching objectives** S1, S3, T20

# Ringlow Park Internet Gardens

Addresses the reader

Present tense

When you enter Ringlow Park Internet Gardens, the first area you come to is the Laptop Glade. This has been lavishly planted with laptops, palmtops and organisers, and is best seen in the spring.

Passive voice

The winding rustic path takes you past the mouse garden. Here, the area has been colonised by the intelli-mouse, completely overtaking the roller mice, who have moved to share the edges of the stream with fading mouse-mats.

Passive voice

Present tense

The formal hardware gardens are a must for visitors in the autumn months. These hold the National Collection of printers, the grey shades of which are shown to best effect in the softer light of September and October. Arranged among the printers is an assortment of desktop PCs, fax machines and cables, while CD-ROMs reflect the light in a stunning end to the tour.

Persuasive

Description

Souvenirs are available in the gift shop.

We hope you have enjoyed your visit, and look forward to welcoming you again.

Closing statement to encourage revisit

## Activity

• Use as a model text to help the children identify the points on page 50.

# Term 3
## Non-fiction

**Recounts**
**Main focus** Revision (model text) (see also page 53)
**NLS teaching objectives** S1, T20, T22

Last week our class visited the Ringlow Park Internet Gardens. We travelled by coach, leaving school at 8 a.m. The journey lasted 3 hours, but we passed the time by doing quizzes.

When we arrived, we all lined up for a photograph before we went in, and then we were put into two groups to explore the gardens. Mrs Wilson led one group, and Mr McKay led the other. We all enjoyed our visit. Mrs Wilson's group spent most of the time in the Laptop Glade, but my group, with Mr McKay, really enjoyed the Mouse Garden most of all. We actually got to stroke some of them. I felt sorry for the old mouse-mats; some of them were very shabby and worn.

When it was time to go home, we waved goodbye to the gardens, each of us very glad we had visited. I enjoyed it so much, I want to be an Internet Gardener when I grow up.

## Activities

- Draw attention to the continued use of the past tense.
- Ask the class to identify the main elements of a recount (who, what, when, where, why and feelings).
- Discuss when children might write write recounts and who might read them.

- Write an imaginary recount of a visit to your fantasy place.

# Term 3
## Non-fiction

**Recounts**
**Main focus** Revision (model text) (see also page 52)
**NLS teaching objectives** S1, T22

When — Last week our class visited the Ringlow Park Internet
Gardens. We travelled by coach, leaving school at
8 a.m. The journey lasted 3 hours, but we passed
the time by doing quizzes.

Who — *our class*
Where — *Ringlow Park Internet*
Past tense — *lasted*

When we arrived, we all lined up for a
photograph before we went in, and then we were
put into two groups to explore the gardens. Mrs
Wilson led one group, and Mr McKay led the other.
We all enjoyed our visit. Mrs Wilson's group spent
most of the time in the Laptop Glade, but my
group, with Mr McKay, really enjoyed the Mouse
Garden most of all. We actually got to stroke some
of them. I felt sorry for the old mouse-mats; some
of them were very shabby and worn.

Sequence vocabulary — *When*
Sequence vocabulary — *then*
Detail — *Mrs Wilson led one group, and Mr McKay led the other.*
Past tense — *enjoyed*

When it was time to go home, we waved
goodbye to the gardens, each of us very glad we
had visited. I enjoyed it so much, I want to be an
Internet Gardener when I grow up.

Sequence vocabulary — *When*
Feelings — *I enjoyed it so much,*

## Activities

- Use as a model text to help the children identify the points on page 52.
- Discuss when children might write recounts and who might read them.

**Instructions**
**Main focus** Revision (model text) (see also page 55)
**NLS teaching objectives** S1, T22

## Writing and printing a document using Word

*Equipment:* Computer, Mouse, Printer, Power cables and Electricity
supply

1. Ensure all cables are plugged into the equipment and connected to the power source.
2. Switch on the computer and printer by pressing the power switch.
3. Move the mouse until the mouse pointer is over the 'Start' button in the bottom left of the screen.
4. Left-click once. The Start menu will appear.
5. Move the mouse pointer up the list until it is over 'New Office Document'.
6. Left-click once with the mouse. A window opens on the screen containing a choice of templates, or formats, for the document.
7. Select the 'Blank Document' template by double-clicking it with the left button on your mouse.
8. Use the keyboard on the computer to type the content of your document.
9. To save your document, hold down the 'Ctrl' key and press 'S' on the keyboard. A new window will open.
10. Type a name for your document in the space at the bottom of the window where it says 'File name'.
11. Left-click the 'OK' button once.
12. Make sure you have some paper in the printer.
13. Hold down 'Ctrl' and press 'P'.
14. The document will then be printed.

### Activities

- Revise the features of an instruction text. Draw attention to the numbered sequence and the command (imperative tense) verb at the beginning of each instruction.
- Discuss when children might write instructions and who might read them.

- Write own instructions related to IT.

**Term 3**
**Non-fiction**

**Instructions**
**Main focus** Revision (annotated model text) (see also page 54)
**NLS teaching objectives** S1, T22

# Writing and printing a document using Word

*Listed at start of instructions*

*Equipment:* Computer, Mouse, Printer, Power cables and Electricity supply

*Numbered sequence*

*Verbs at beginning of sentence*

1. Ensure all cables are plugged into the equipment and connected to the power source.
2. Switch on the computer and printer by pressing the power switch.
3. Move the mouse until the mouse pointer is over the 'Start' button in the bottom left of the screen.
4. Left-click once. The Start menu will appear.
5. Move the mouse pointer up the list until it is over 'New Office Document'.
6. Left-click once with the mouse. A window opens on the screen containing a choice of templates, or formats, for the document.
7. Select the 'Blank Document' template by double-clicking it with the left button on your mouse.
8. Use the keyboard on the computer to type the content of your document.
9. To save your document, hold down the 'Ctrl' key and press 'S' on the keyboard. A new window will open.
10. Type a name for your document in the space at the bottom of the window where it says 'File name'.
11. Left-click the 'OK' button once.
12. Make sure you have some paper in the printer.
13. Hold down 'Ctrl' and press 'P'.
14. The document will then be printed.

## Activities

- Use as a model text to help the children identify the points on page 54.
- Discuss when children might write instructions and who might read them.

## Term 3
## Non-fiction

**Reports**
**Main focus** Revision (model text) (see also page 57)
**NLS teaching objectives** S1, T22

## The computer mouse

A computer mouse is a pad, usually attached to the computer by a wire, that enables the user to move a cursor around the computer screen. Few people can imagine using a computer without a mouse. It was invented in 1968 by Douglas Engelbart. He had been a radar technician during World War II, and had a vision of people being able to interact with personal computers in the 1960s.

The first computer mouse was called the 'x-y position indicator'. No one knows who christened it 'mouse', but today everyone knows it by that name. Most computer mice have a ball on the base, which rolls as it is moved around, and two to three buttons to click, sending information through the wire to the computer.

Recent inventions have added mice that use radio technology. These are wireless mice, so many of today's mice have lost their tails. However, futher inventions include a device that uses a reflective dot which can be put on your finger or even your nose. Another is a wand called 'Kat'. So soon the Kat may chase away the mouse completely.

### Activities

- Draw attention to conventions of giving a general statement, then more detailed description.
- Discuss when children might write reports and who might read them.

- Write own report on an IT-related topic.

**Term 3**
**Non-fiction**

**Reports**
**Main focus** Revision (annotated model text) (see also page 56)
**NLS teaching objectives** S1, T22

## The computer mouse

Definition

Generalization

A computer mouse is a pad, usually attached to the computer by a wire, that enables the user to move a cursor around the computer screen. Few people can imagine using a computer without a mouse. It was invented in 1968 by Douglas Engelbart. He had been a radar technician during World War II, and had a vision of people being able to interact with personal computers in the 1960s.

Statement of fact

Technical terms

The first computer mouse was called the 'x-y position indicator'. No one knows who christened it 'mouse', but today everyone knows it by that name. Most computer mice have a ball on the base, which rolls as it is moved around, and two to three buttons to click, sending information through the wire to the computer.

Technical terms

Description

Description

Recent inventions have added mice that use radio technology. These are wireless mice, so many of today's mice have lost their tails. However, futher inventions include a device that uses a reflective dot which can be put on your finger or even your nose. Another is a wand called 'Kat'. So soon the Kat may chase away the mouse completely.

Technical terms

**Activities**

- Use as a model text to help the children identify the points on page 56.
- Discuss when children might write reports and who might read them.

**Term 3**
**Non-fiction**

**Explanations**
**Main focus** Revision (model text) (see also page 59)
**NLS teaching objectives** S1, T20, T22

## How the computer mouse works

Computer mice are an integral part of computer use today. Although invented in 1968, it took until 1984 for mice to be used by the general public. The mouse enables you to move your cursor around the computer screen, or activate a program or instruction.

The main function of a mouse is to sense the motion of your hand, and send this information to the computer.

*Inside story*
Most mice use five components to send signals to your computer:

1. A ball inside the mouse touches the surface of your desk and rolls as the mouse moves.
2. Two rollers inside the mouse touch the ball and detect direction.
3. Each roller is connected to a shaft which spins a disk with holes in it.
4. On each side of the disk is an infrared LED* and sensor.

    a. The infrared sensor detects pulses of light from the LED as they beam through the holes in the disk.
    b. The rate of these light pulses tells the computer about the speed and distance the mouse travels.

5. A processor chip reads the pulses and turns them into binary data, which is sent to the computer.

If you move a mouse very quickly, it may travel 25 mm or more in one-fortieth of a second, and detect more than 41 pulses of light in that time.

* Light emitting diode

## Activities

- Draw attention to the layout and the sequence.
- Discuss when children might write explanations and who might read them.

- Use as model for writing own explanation.

**Term 3**
**Non-fiction**

**Explanations**
**Main focus** Revision (model text) (see also page 58)
**NLS teaching objectives** S1, T20, T22

**How the computer mouse works** —— What is being explained

—— Generalized participants

(Computer mice) are an integral part of computer use today. Although invented in 1968, it took until 1984 for mice to be used by the general public. The mouse enables you to move your cursor around the computer screen, or activate a program or instruction.

The main function of a mouse is to sense the motion of your hand, and send this information to the computer.

Sub-—— *Inside story*
heading Most mice use five components to send signals to your computer: —— Action verbs

Numbered sequence

1. A ball inside the mouse (touches) the surface of your desk and (rolls) as the mouse moves.
2. Two rollers inside the mouse touch the ball and detect direction.
3. Each roller is connected to a shaft which spins a disk with holes in it.
4. On each side of the disk is an infrared LED* and sensor.

   a. The infrared sensor detects pulses of light from the LED as they beam through the holes in the disk.
   b. The rate of these light pulses tells the computer about the speed and distance the mouse travels.

5. A processor chip reads the pulses and turns them into binary data, which is sent to the computer.

If you move a mouse very quickly, it may travel 25 mm or more in one-fortieth of a second, and detect more than 41 pulses of light in that time.

Fascinating fact to close explanation

\* Light emitting diode

**Activities**

- Use as a model text to help the children identify the points raised on page 58.
- Discuss when children might write explanations and who might read them.

**Term 3**
**Non-fiction**

**Persuasive writing**
**Main focus** Revision (model text) (see also page 61)
**NLS teaching objectives** S1, T20, T22

# EASY PEASY MICE

- Does your mouse ever let you down?

- Are you tired of lazy mice?

- Would you like a super-responsive rodent?

**Easy Peasy Mice are the newest, the best, the sleekest mice around.**

**Call for a free demonstration.**

**DON'T DELAY, CALL TODAY**

## Activities

- Draw attention to 'Attention-grabbing' devices, rhetorical questions and the call to action.
- Discuss when children might write persuasively and who might read it.

- Create an advert for another piece of computer hardware.

## Term 3
### Non-fiction

**Persuasive writing**
**Main focus** Revision (model text) (see also page 60)
**NLS teaching objectives** S1, T20, T22

Grabs attention

# EASY PEASY MICE

Rhetorical questions

- Does your mouse ever let you down?
  - Are you tired of lazy mice?
- Would you like a super-responsive rodent?

**Easy Peasy Mice are the (newest) the (best) the (sleekest) mice around.**

Superlatives

**Call for a free demonstration.**

**DON'T DELAY, (CALL) TODAY**

Addresses the reader personally

Command verbs

## Activities

- Use as a model text to help the children identify the points raised on page 60.
- Discuss when children might write persuasively and who might read it.